US MILITARY EQUIPMENT
AND VEHICLES

US SPECIAL OPERATIONS FORCES EQUIPMENT AND VEHICLES

BY ELIZABETH PAGEL-HOGAN

CONTENT CONSULTANT
DIANE ZORRI, PhD
NON-RESIDENT SENIOR FELLOW
JOINT SPECIAL OPERATIONS UNIVERSITY

Kids Core
An Imprint of Abdo Publishing
abdobooks.com

abdobooks.com

Printed in the United States of America, North Mankato, Minnesota
052021
092021

THIS BOOK CONTAINS
RECYCLED MATERIALS

Cover Photo: Cpl. William Chockey/US Marine Corps/Defense Visual Information Distribution Service
Interior Photos: Senior Airman Jasmonet Jackson/US Air Force/Defense Visual Information Distribution Service, 4–5; Red Line Editorial, 7; Sgt. 1st Class Jeremy D. Crisp/US Army, 8; Staff Sgt. Elizabeth Pena/US Army/Defense Visual Information Distribution Service, 10; Lance Cpl. Israel Chincio/US Marine Corps/Defense Visual Information Distribution Service, 12–13; Ryan White/US Air National Guard/Defense Visual Information Distribution Service, 14; Senior Airman Justine Rho/US Air Force/Defense Visual Information Distribution Service, 16; Spc. Ryan Lucas/Defense Visual Information Distribution Service, 18–19; Senior Airman Julianne Showalter/Defense Visual Information Distribution Service, 20; Staff Sgt. Timothy Pruitt/Texas State Guard/Defense Visual Information Distribution Service, 21; Gunnery Sgt. Ismael Pena/US Marine Corps/Defense Visual Information Distribution Service, 23; SOF AT&L/Defense Visual Information Distribution Service, 24; Staff Sgt. John Bainter/US Air Force/Defense Visual Information Distribution Service, 26, 29 (bottom); Lance Cpl. Samantha A. Barajas/US Marine Corps/Defense Visual Information Distribution Service, 28; Michael Wood/Stocktrek Images/Alamy, 29 (top)

Editor: Katharine Hale
Series Designer: Jake Nordby

Library of Congress Control Number: 2020948454

Publisher's Cataloging-in-Publication Data

Names: Pagel-Hogan, Elizabeth, author.
Title: US special operations forces equipment and vehicles / by Elizabeth Pagel-Hogan
Description: Minneapolis, Minnesota : Abdo Publishing, 2022 | Series: US military equipment and vehicles | Includes online resources and index.
Identifiers: ISBN 9781532195488 (lib. bdg.) | ISBN 9781644946213 (pbk.) | ISBN 9781098215798 (ebook)
Subjects: LCSH: Special forces (Military science)--Juvenile literature. | Commando troops--Juvenile literature. | Vehicles, Military--Juvenile literature. | Military supplies--Juvenile literature. | Military paraphernalia--Juvenile literature.
Classification: DDC 623.7--dc23

CONTENTS

The AC-130W Stinger II is one of many aircraft used by US Special Operations Forces.

CHAPTER 1

MEET THE SOF

The loud growl of a plane engine fills the air. It is an AC-130W Stinger II. This plane carries soldiers who are part of the US Special Operations Command. The plane is helping other soldiers monitor a dangerous area.

The huge gray machine thunders through the sky. The Stinger has weapons. It also has cameras. Cameras can record information on the ground from far away. This information can help soldiers complete their mission.

Special Operations Forces

US Special Operations Forces (SOF) are special groups of military members. They are trained to carry out important missions. There are SOF units in different branches of the military. For example, US Army SOF groups include the Green Berets, Rangers, and Night Stalkers. US Navy SOF groups include the Sea, Air, and Land (SEAL) Teams. The US Air Force and Marines have SOF units too.

Special Operations Forces Units

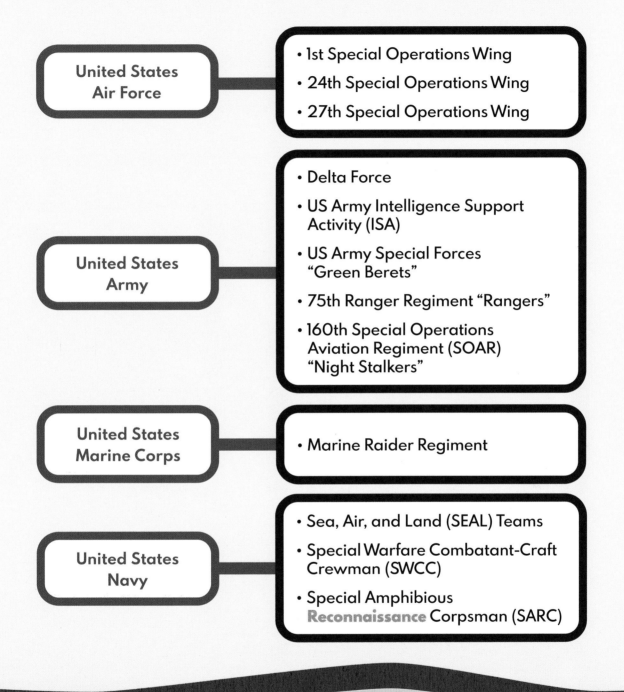

United States Air Force
- 1st Special Operations Wing
- 24th Special Operations Wing
- 27th Special Operations Wing

United States Army
- Delta Force
- US Army Intelligence Support Activity (ISA)
- US Army Special Forces "Green Berets"
- 75th Ranger Regiment "Rangers"
- 160th Special Operations Aviation Regiment (SOAR) "Night Stalkers"

United States Marine Corps
- Marine Raider Regiment

United States Navy
- Sea, Air, and Land (SEAL) Teams
- Special Warfare Combatant-Craft Crewman (SWCC)
- Special Amphibious Reconnaissance Corpsman (SARC)

There are many SOF units across the branches of the military. These are just a few.

The Green Berets were named the first official SOF unit of the US Army in 1952.

SOF members go through difficult training. They learn survival skills. They learn new languages and customs. SOF members handle many different missions. They may gather information. Sometimes they train soldiers from different countries. Other times they rescue people who are trapped.

How to Join the Green Berets

To qualify for the Green Berets, a person needs to be an active duty soldier. The soldier must be a US citizen. Soldiers must have a high school diploma. They must be between 20 and 32 years old. They must pass a physical fitness test and a knowledge and ability test.

SOF units train with soldiers around the world to prepare for emergency situations.

SOF members need special equipment and vehicles to complete their missions. Some use boats and breathing equipment. Others use ground vehicles and night-vision goggles. SOF members are used to handling difficult challenges. Their equipment and vehicles have to be ready for anything too.

SOF soldiers sometimes test new equipment. Captain Brian McNally said:

> Any time Soldiers and their leaders get involved in operational testing, they have the opportunity to use, work with, and offer up their own suggestions on pieces of equipment.

Source: Rod Manke. "Special Operations Command Soldiers Test RA-1 Double Bag Static Line Parachute System, USASOC C-27J." *US Army*, 17 Oct. 2018, army.mil. Accessed 14 May 2020.

What's the Big Idea?

Read this quote carefully. What is its main idea? Explain how the main idea is supported by details.

Many night-vision goggles have a green tint.

CHAPTER 2

SPECIAL EQUIPMENT

SOF soldiers use advanced equipment. Special equipment helps soldiers complete important missions safely. One example is night-vision goggles (NVGs). NVGs help soldiers see in the dark.

GPNVGs have four lenses, which allows soldiers to see more while wearing them.

Delta Force soldiers are part of the army. They use Ground **Panoramic** Night Vision Goggles (GPNVGs). Some NVGs only have two lenses. This limits how much a soldier can see. But GPNVGs have four lenses. This gives soldiers a panoramic view. They can see better to complete their missions.

Water Equipment

Some SOF missions happen near water. SOF sailors such as SEALs can use the LAR V

Draeger rebreather to breathe underwater. The rebreather captures and recycles all of a sailor's air. Sailors can move underwater without being seen because no air is released into the water. This means there are no bubbles. The device also removes carbon dioxide from the exhaled air. Then the air is safe for the sailor to breathe back in.

Hiding from Radar

US Army Night Stalkers fly the MH-47G Chinook helicopter. This large helicopter has infrared exhaust suppressors. Exhaust from the engine is hot. This equipment mixes the exhaust with cooler air. This makes it harder for infrared scanners to spot the helicopter.

RA-1 parachutes, *pictured*, replaced the older MC-4 parachute system.

Air Equipment

Many US Army Rangers start missions by jumping out of a plane. These soldiers use an RA-1 Advanced Ram Air Parachute System to safely travel to the ground. This parachute is designed for high altitude, low opening (HALO) jumps. HALO jumps are when soldiers jump out of a plane while it is high in the air. The soldiers only open their parachutes when they are close to the ground. The RA-1 parachute works even in extreme weather. It has a GPS device that helps soldiers know where they are. It also has an oxygen mask to help soldiers breathe.

Explore Online

Visit the website below. Does it give any new information about SOF equipment that wasn't in Chapter Two?

Special Forces Weapons, Equipment, and Vehicles

abdocorelibrary.com/sof-equipment -vehicles

Various SOF units use slightly different models of the GMV.

CHAPTER **3**

SOF ON THE MOVE

Special forces such as Green Berets need to move quickly over all kinds of terrain. The Ground Mobility Vehicle (GMV) is perfect for the job. It can carry troops and their equipment over rough ground. Helicopters can deliver the GMV to the mission area.

Dirt bikes and motorcycles allow SOF soldiers to drive in places larger vehicles cannot.

Sometimes the GMV is too big and bulky. Then soldiers rely on motorcycles. Some SOF members use the Kawasaki KLR 250-D8 to move quickly in narrow places, such as a city. The headlights have **infrared** lights. This means only people with NVGs can see them. It also has a muffler that hides the noise of the engine.

Another important ground vehicle is the Light Medium Tactical Vehicle (LMTV) "War Pig." The War Pig is a modified LMTV. Green Berets

A regular LMTV, *pictured*, has an enclosed cab, but a War Pig is open-air.

drive War Pigs. These trucks carry fuel and other supplies to soldiers operating far from the main base. The truck has weapons placed on the front and back. These protect the soldiers inside.

Some special forces soldiers do **reconnaissance** missions. They might use an M1161 Light Strike Vehicle, or "Growler." This is a small jeep. The wheel rims help it keep moving even with flat tires. The seats have Kevlar padding that can stop bullets. The Growler can be carried by a helicopter and driven off-road.

Water Vehicles

Navy SEALs use a mini submarine for secret missions. It is called the SEAL Delivery Vehicle (SDV). It can hold six SEALs. It carries them into dangerous areas without being spotted. The SDV can move through shallow water where larger submarines cannot go. It travels almost silently through the water.

US Marines also use CRRC for missions.

SEALs use Combat Rubber Raiding Craft (CRRC) as well. These boats can be inflated quickly. They have motors but can also be paddled to move quietly. The boats can be carried by helicopter, plane, and submarine.

The MH-6M is not armed. Its main purpose is to transport SOF soldiers.

Air Vehicles

The US Army Night Stalkers fly a special helicopter. It is called the MH-6M Little Bird. The MH-6M can bring SOF troops into a city. It is small enough to fly down a narrow street. The helicopter can land on a small roof. Little Bird fuel tanks are bulletproof.

Special Messages

The 193rd Special Operations Wing is part of the US Air National Guard. It uses the EC-130 Commando Solo plane. This plane has radio and television equipment. It can broadcast messages by radio and television when it flies over an area.

The US Air Force began using the Osprey in the 2000s.

Another air vehicle is the CV-22 Osprey. This plane is used by some US Air Force Special Operations Wings. The Osprey has rotors that can tilt. This means the plane can hover, take off, and land like a helicopter. It can also fly like a plane. It can deliver SOF soldiers to an area. It can also be used to search an area to find people in danger.

SOF units are highly trained groups of soldiers. They travel into dangerous areas. They go underwater, fly in the air, and cover any kind of ground. Special equipment and vehicles help SOF members complete their missions around the world.

Further Evidence

Visit the website below. Does it give any new evidence about the Little Bird to support Chapter Three?

Fact Sheet: A/MH-6M Little Bird Helicopters

abdocorelibrary.com/sof-equipment -vehicles

IMPORTANT GEAR

M1161 "Growler"

- Kevlar-padded seats stop bullets

- Can move with flat tires

- Can be carried by a helicopter

LAR V Draeger Rebreather

- Used by Navy SEALs
- Recycles air so there are no bubbles
- Can be used in rivers and streams

CV-22 Osprey

- Has tilting rotors
- Can lift off like a helicopter
- Can fly fast like a plane

Glossary

altitude
the height of something in the air above sea level

broadcast
to send out by radio or television

carbon dioxide
a gas made of carbon and oxygen that humans breathe out

infrared
a type of light that cannot be seen with the human eye

panoramic
showing a wide or full view

reconnaissance
the act of collecting information

terrain
the surface of land or ground and its features

Online Resources

To learn more about SOF equipment and vehicles, visit our free resource websites below.

Visit **abdocorelibrary.com** or scan this QR code for free Common Core resources for teachers and students, including vetted activities, multimedia, and booklinks, for deeper subject comprehension.

Visit **abdobooklinks.com** or scan this QR code for free additional online weblinks for further learning. These links are routinely monitored and updated to provide the most current information available.

Learn More

Abdo, Kenny. *Navy SEALs*. Abdo Publishing, 2019.

Bassier, Emma. *Military Gear*. Abdo Publishing, 2020.

London, Martha. *Military Animals*. Abdo Publishing, 2020.

Index

About the Author

Elizabeth Pagel-Hogan is a children's author from Pittsburgh, Pennsylvania. She's also the daughter of a US Navy veteran.